BRECHT

OR BEGINNERS

WRITERS AND READERS PUBLISHING, INCORPORATED
One West 125th Street
Dr. Martin Luther King, Jr. Blvd.
New York, N.Y. 10027
Text & Illustrations Copyright © 1984 La Decouverte
Concept and Design Copyright © 1984 Writers and
Readers Publishing, Inc.
Cover Design: Chris Hyde

A Writers and Readers Documentary Comic Book
Copyright © 1984
ISBN 0 86316 100 6
2 3 4 5 6 7 8 9 0
Manufactured in the United States of America
Beginners Documentary Comic books are published by
Writers and Readers Publishing, Inc. Its trademark, con-
sisting of the words "For Beginners, Writers and Readers
Documentary Comic Books" and the portrayal of a seal
bearing the words "Beginners Documentary Comic
Books" and Writers and Readers logo, is registered in the
U.S. Patent and Trademark Office and in other countries.

Carthage fought three wars. After the first, the great city was still powerful and after the second it was still habitable. After the third, however, it had disappeared without trace.

September 1951

CONTENTS

Acknowledgements

We would like to thank AGET Language Services for their translation and Dr. John White of King's College, London for his corrections and suggestions.

Also thanks to Linda Briggs for her editorial work and to Benny Kandler for his paste-up.

ACT 1 : Youth

Mr and Mrs Brecht take great pleasure in informing you of the birth of their son

Bertolt Eugen

Bertholt Brecht was born in Germany o
the end of the 19th century when impe
Britain and Russia were dividing up the
out for new sources of raw materials at

Though eager to establish his own colonial
empire, the sabre-rattling young Kaiser,
Wilhelm II, had to make do with the left-overs: a
few bits of land in Africa and the odd atoll in the
Pacific.

6

ebruary 1898, in the town of Augsburg in Bavaria. This was
was at its height and the great colonial powers, France,
between them. Their expanding economies were crying
ce.

All this was costing more than it was
bringing in. So, it didn't take him
long to decide that a war in Europe
would be a better bet.

His father, Friedrich Brecht, who worked as a clerk in a paper mill.

His mother, Sophie Brecht, née Brezing.

When I was at school, I realized that the best way to get higher marks wasn't to rub out the teacher's corrections but to add more where there was no reason for them. This was embarrassing for the teacher who had to give me a better mark...

Bert first declared himself an anti-militarist at the age of 18. In a school essay on Horace's line, 'dulce et decorum est pro patria mori', he wrote:

'Whether it comes in bed or on the field of battle, death is always painful. It's only the empty-headed who talk about laying down their lives and they are the first to run as soon as death approaches.'

For this rebellion against the approved line, he came close to being expelled.

The First World War, started by the General Staff c to test new weapons. As the conflict spreads this c about nationalism.

'War is like a spa-water cure.'
Hindenburg (1847–1934) Murderer-in-Chief (1914–18) then President of the Reich in 1925.

erman army, is initially used by the arms industry
?s into a roaring trade unperturbed by qualms

While millions of men are being killed by bombs and gas at the front, Wilhelm II refuses to sign an armistice, though the war has long since been lost...

To avoid conscription, Brecht enrols at the University of Munich to study medicine. Soon afterwards, he does his military service in the VD section of an army hospital in Augsburg. In the 'Legend of the Dead Soldier' (soon to earn him the hatred of the Fascists), he denounces the last-ditch mentality of the German military.

Fight on! Never surrender! ...More tea Ludendorff?

He is rooted out and sent to the front on the orders of the Emperor...

Ballad of the Dead Soldier

The soldier was stinking with decay
so a priest goes on before
to give him incense of his way
that he may stink no more.

In front the band with oom-pah-pah
intones a rousing march
The soldier does like the handbook says
and flicks his legs from his arse.

They paint his shroud with the black-white-red
of the old imperial flag
with so much colour it covers up
that bloody spattered rag.

Defeat of Germany

14

Ties of friendship and shared artistic leanings bring Brecht together with an old schoolmate, the painter **Caspar Neher.**

29.12.1917

Dear Cas!

Nothing is happening in art. I'm for closing down all the theatres – for artistic reasons. There will be no art until the last theatre-goer has been hung with the guts of the last actor....

I, Bertold Brecht, came out of the black forests.
My mother moved me into the cities as I lay
Inside her body. And the coldness of the forests
Will be inside me till my dying day.

In the asphalt city I'm at home. From the very start
Provided with every last sacrament:
With newspapers. And tobacco. And brandy
To the end mistrustful, lazy and content.

Just between ourselves, it's not particularly brilliant!

hasengasse

He is drawn to circuses and fairs. With a high voice, he sings ballads and plays the guitar. He chain-smokes cigars and is a byword for coarseness. Despairing of the provincialism of Augsburg, he goes to Munich...

Munich, at this time, is the centre for Bohemian life and the German avant-garde. Brecht spends more time in writers' cafés and bars than on his studies. He meets **Frank Wedekind**, the writer and singer whom he admires most.

'Morals is the best business in the world!'

Life is a helter-skelter.

Wedekind (1864–1918) is a fearless satirist of philistinism and its double standards. He created the famous character Lulu who, in several plays, embodies the unconquerable and fateful sexual instinct. The animality of human nature is also the central theme of Brecht's first play, *Baal*.

In 1918 Brecht writes the first version of *Baal* as a reaction against Expressionist theatre. Baal is a poet who sings his verses in sleazy joints. Baal's debauchery and his insatiable appetite are his response to an entourage that feeds off his genius...

Baal, you fat slob. When you die, you'll be too heavy to fly to heaven!

Burp! Yum, yum!

If you don't stop stuffing yourself, Baal, you're going to explode!

I'd like to hear the explosion.*

For him, as for Rimbaud, art is life itself. Brecht argues against any metaphysical view of human nature. For him, there is no such thing as unchangeable human characteristics.

* Fassbinder playing Baal in one of his first films.

Baal

Baal grew up within the whiteness of the womb
With the sky already large and pale and calm
Naked, young, endlessly marvellous
As Baal loved it when he came to us.

Once a woman, Baal says, gives her all
She'll have nothing more, so let her go!
Other men would represent no risk at all.
Even Baal is scared of babies, though.

Baal watches the vultures in the star-shot sky
Hovering patiently to see when Baal will die.
Sometimes Baal shams dead. The vultures swoop.
Baal, without a word, will dine on vulture soup.

The other determining influence on Brecht in Munich is that of the Bavarian comic, **Karl Valentin**, whose sketches portray the human animal in all its forms...

'This man is the most complex of satirists. His humour is very dry so that you can carry on drinking and smoking while at the same time you are shaking inside with none too benevolent laughter.'

It is from Valentin that Brecht gets his taste for biting satire and the grotesque.

Under Valentin's influence, Brecht writes a series of short farces in the style of the French 'sotie'. The funniest of these is undoubtedly *A Petit Bourgeois' Wedding*, a satirical parody in which the guests lose their affability during the course of the reception as the husband's do-it-yourself furniture crumples under them. The bride is chatted up by one of the guests and the couple then have a row. The play comes to a close with laughter as the last piece of furniture collapses in the darkness, taking with it the pillars of the traditional family.

Meanwhile, workers' and soldiers' councils have taken power in Germany.

▽

What is a council of workers and soldiers?

▽

In Russia workers and soldiers of the Soviets have direct elections to send their representatives to local and regional councils and right up to the Supreme Council. Such representatives delegate 'People's Commissars' to carry out governmental missions.

Kiel

Hamburg   LÜBECK

Bremen

HANOVER

Berlin

Cologne

Munich

In November 1918 sailors at Kiel mutinied (against an order to attack a superior force of English ships).

Councils of workers and soldiers are formed in the large towns and, within days, the revolt directed by the Spartacists has reached Berlin!...

Spartacus!

Dissident militants from the majority Social-Democratic party gather around **Karl Liebknecht** and **Rosa Luxemburg**. They call themselves Spartacus and only they rise up against the war.

'The principal enemy of the German people is to be found in Germany itself. It is the same cliques who sow discord between nations and turn it into money!!'

'To avoid further fratricidal wars, the banks, heavy industry and great estates must belong to the people...'

KARL LIEBKNECHT
1871 - 1919

ROSA LUXEMBURG
1870 - 1919

The Spartacist movement has taken root in many German cities. I will follow it closely but I won't take part in it...

So, Mr Artist, you've got nothing better to do than comment on events?

24

Kurt Eisner, prime minister of the Republic of Councils of Bavaria, is assassinated. This provokes an uprising which is quickly suppressed.

Brecht claims to have been a delegate to one of the worker councils during this period and to have concealed in his own home a revolutionary who was being hunted down by the Freikorps.

Drums in the Night

is his second play. Originally entitled *Spartacus*, it is set during the abortive revolution in Germany. On 18 November the soldier Kragler, who was supposed to have died in Africa, returns to Berlin.

He finds that his fiancée, Anna, daughter of a war profiteer, has been made pregnant by someone else to whom she has to get married. It is the eve of the Spartacist revolt, but Kragler stays out of things in order to win back Anna.

Brecht goes to show his first plays to **Leon Feuchtwanger** (1884–1958). The future author of *Jew Süss* and of a good number of historical novels already enjoys a solid reputation.

Feuchtwanger is so taken with Brecht's heavy Swabian accent and general demeanour that he even introduces him into one of his novels. It is the beginning of a long collaboration and friendship. Indeed, it's thanks to Feuchtwanger that the play Brecht shows him, *Drums in the Night*, is put on in Munich.

At this time, Bert is drama critic for the Augsburg paper *Der Volkswille*. The leading lights of Expressionism are very much in vogue and it is this movement which is his favourite target. Their idealistic view of man and the false pathos of the characters is the opposite of Brecht's materialistic outlook.

Meanwhile, he has to pay a 100 mark fine for insulting an actress who, from all accounts, had no talent anyway.

Berlin

The revolution having drowned in its own blood, right wing extremism is gaining ground. In Berlin there is poverty and violence. Political assassinations are commonplace.

In the arts, the same moral poison is present. At this time, the Berlin 'Dadaists' are the most politicized of the avant-garde movements.
In their demonstrations and events, they attack both bourgeois art and political institutions with the same vehemence.

Brecht shares their taste for heresy... and makes a name for himself by desecrating the theatre. The very idea of pure art drives him into fits of rage. To counter this, he advocates gaiety in art.

'Purity of art has nothing to do with how clean the subject matter is. As with women, innocence comes in many degrees. It's not something one can lose but rather something that one can acquire.'

1921 – Brecht arrives in Berlin. His reputation as a merciless critic has preceded him. In the evenings, he frequents literary cafés and society parties but no one takes up the challenge of producing his plays. He becomes friendly with the young playwright, **Arnold Bronnen.**

The Volksbühne, modelled on the Théâtre Antoine, offers cheap seats in the hope of bringing the theatre within everyone's reach.
At the opposite extreme, the Deutsches Theater under Max Reinhardt is a temple of luxury with neo-baroque productions that are world-famous. Brecht's polemics against the 'theatre of illusion' are aimed essentially against Reinhardt.

Bert moves in with Bronnen. Soon, however, Bronnen's pay for his work as a clerk is no longer enough to feed them.

Leave a bit for tomorrow, Arnold!

OK Bert.

SARDINES A L'HUILE

In January the undernourished Brecht goes into hospital....

'Hospital is a good place for a young author to study!'

Today's menu: Vitamin A, B, C, D, etc...

Brecht quickly recovers... With Bronnen, he tries another tactic: they publicize each other's work.

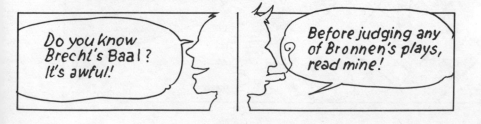

Do you know Brecht's Baal? It's awful!

Before judging any of Bronnen's plays, read mine!

The only art to come out of the city so far is jazz and the films of Charlie Chaplin!

His dream, as for a whole generation of artists, is the great cities of the USA.
Brecht has great admiration for Chaplin who he believes has found a really modern form of expression.

This first experience of the daily struggle is echoed in a new p

In the Jungle of Cities

Inspired by Upton Sinclair's book, *The Jungle*, Brecht sets his play in the Chicago of 1912.

'You will see a mysterious contest between two men. You will see a family come from the plains and disappear into the jungle of the city. Share in their human involvement, judge the adversaries with an impartial eye and keep your whole attention for the final round.'

Schlink, a rich timber merchant, is attracted by a young libraria

rga, and forces him into a spiritual battle.

But the social struggle no longer allows for a victor, not even for communication.

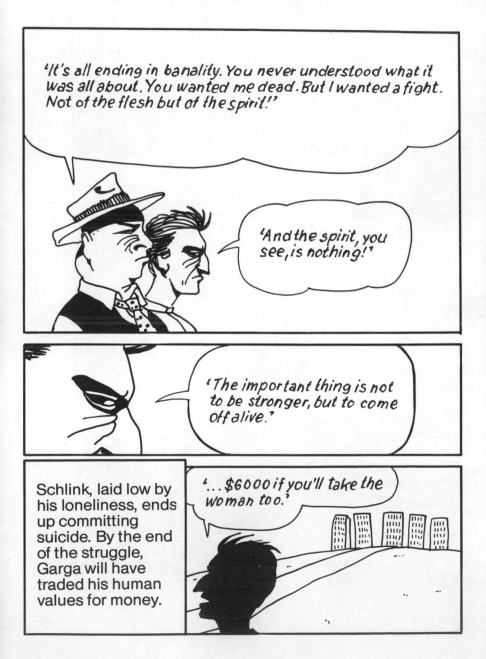

In the autumn, Bronnen introduces to Brecht a young Viennese actress, **Helene Weigel.** A few days later Brecht moves in with her into her Berlin studio.
She is to be his favourite actress and will be the inspiration for his principal feminine roles, including that of mother of his children: Stefan and Barbara.

Paula Banholzer: his first fiancée.

Marianne Zoff: his first wife.

In order to survive, Bronnen and Brecht enter a competition for the best film scenario. They win the first prize of 10,000 marks but, unfortunately, by the time it is paid, it is worth nothing. Inflation is raging.

The only amusing thing at the time was going to pay your taxes.

So what's going on?

Under the Treaty of Versailles, the Weimar Republic has to pay out 20 billion gold marks and to give up vast territories to the east (conditions which Hitler is soon to use as a pretext for his policy of annexation).

For the population, it's a race against the clock:

In 1920 inflation is running at 240%.

In 1922 inflation is at 2,400% compared with the previous year.

In 1923 it is almost at its peak as French and Belgian troops occupy the Ruhr. A general strike is launched and nationalist propaganda gains ground.

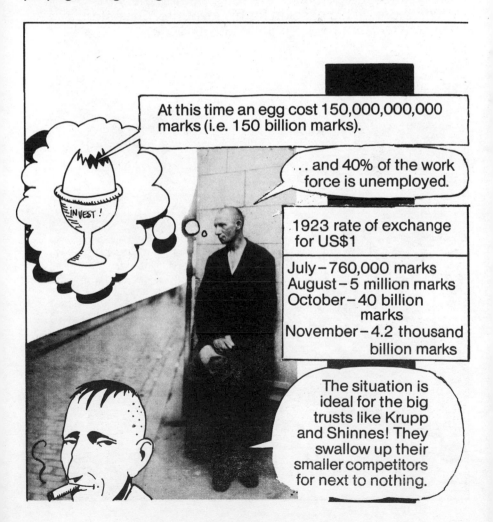

The Life of Edward II of England

With the help of Feuchtwanger, Brecht adapts the work of Marlowe (1564–1593) for the Munich chamber players. It is his first successful production. Brecht demystifies the person of the King, putting the stress much more on his passion for his favourite, Gaveston, a passion which throws England into civil war.

During the rehearsals Brecht works on physical expression. He insists on events being shown as they are without sentimentality and false statements.

It was during one of these rehearsals that the idea of epic theatre came to Brecht. He was having trouble portraying the soldiers for the battle of Killingworth.
How should they be presented?
What was special about them?

This remark was the turning point. The soldiers' faces were covered with chalk and the style of the play was established...

In 1923 in Munich, Hitler, with a group of local war veterans (and future Nazis) attempts a *putsch* in the **Burgerbraukeller** where the Bavarian government is holding a function...

Hitler is arrested and imprisoned in the fortress of **Landsberg.** His party is banned.

Hitler will later be released and will quickly re-establish his party.

Shortly before, Brecht had invited Bronnen to Munich where the two friends went to the Krone circus to listen to Hitler.

Brecht comes to an early verdict on this pantomime. Dismayed by the parades of SA storm-troopers, he realizes to what an extent contemporary man can be manipulated. This is to result in ...

... a new play! Which is:

MAN EQUALS MAN

Brecht feels the need to use new dramatic forms. In this comedy, for the first time, he uses songs and commentaries addressed directly at the audience to create a distancing effect.

Be patient, we are on the way towards an epic theatre.

'Mr Bertolt Brecht affirms that:
A man is a man.
And that's something we would all agree with him on.
He also proves that you can make of a man what you will.
Here, this evening, you will see a man taken to bits like a car.

Galy Gay is a docker in India. Sent out by his wife to get fish, he falls in with three soldiers. They persuade him to take the place of one of their comrades who is being held in a pagoda that he has been looting.
Once in uniform, Galy Gay is unrecognizable.

Peter Lorre, actor.

My name is nobody.

There's today's personality for you!

Having shed his individuality, Galy Gay is rapidly transformed into a fighting machine. (A good example of social conformism!)

During this period, Brecht is an avid sports' fan.

All our hopes rest on the sporting public – 15,000 people from every social class, paying good money for their seats and getting good value for it... The theatre-going public is corrupt because neither the theatre nor the audience has the slightest idea of what should go on. In the stadium, people know exactly what the price of a ticket is going to get them: trained men display their particular skills and look as though they enjoy it... There's really no reason why the theatre shouldn't be such good sport...

His scorn for opulent audiences is well known. For him, the bourgeois theatre is an insipid diversion, hence his admiration for boxing.

Whet the appetites of the audience, their fighting spirit, their analytical powers...

'All those who've lost their reflexes get out!'

He becomes friends with the boxer **Samson-Köner** and writes his biography.

You're a great guy!

You're quick and light on your feet ... I'll send my actors to study your style!...

In 1927 Brecht is on the panel of judges for a poetry competition. Over 400 poets submit their work but in them Brecht can find nothing but sentimentality, hypocrisy and ignorance of the real world.

In the end he awards the prize to a piece taken out of a sports paper. Entitled 'Hey! Hey! The Iron Man', it's a tribute in greeting-card verse to a champion cyclist.

Throughout his life, detective stories (preferably English ones) are his favourite bedtime reading. Just as in the theatre, what interests him is not the psychology of the characters but the logical development of the plot.

'Who-dunnits encourage logical thought and root out false sentiment!!'

'That lot write for geriatrics!'

STEFAN GEORGE

FRANZ WERFEL

RAINER M. RILKE

THOMAS MANN

?

Brecht's pursuit of the trivial is his reaction against the literary traditions of a decadent bourgeoisie.

Brecht meets the sociologist, **Fritz Sternberg** at Schlichter's restaurant and from him gets a taste for Marxism.

'The decadence of the drama is a historical necessity, a consequence of the transition from the individual to the collective...'

The fact that the modern world can no longer find a place within established dramatic forms means only that the forms themselves are no longer adapted to our world.

Really?

Brecht's interest in new dramatic forms draws him inevitably to **Erwin Piscator** (1893–1966).

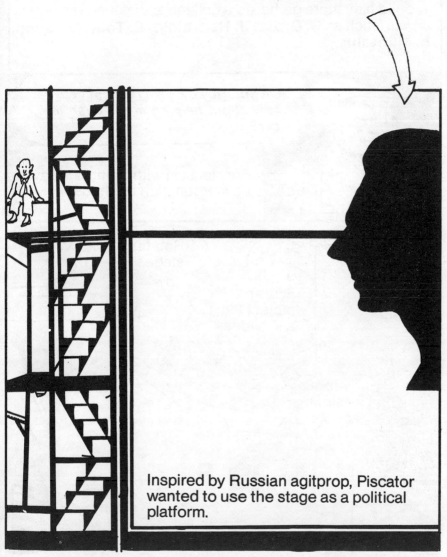

Inspired by Russian agitprop, Piscator wanted to use the stage as a political platform.

Piscator had worked at the Volksbühne as a producer but had been sacked for adopting Communist positions. Subsequently, he had opened his own theatre on the Nollendorfplatz.

Around him, there gathered a collective of young radical artists (such as **G. Grosz, J. Heartfield, E. Toller, F. Jung, E. Mühsam**).

OK you guys. As we're a collective, how about helping me to push my car?...

Bert joins in with them to study new production methods.

Rotating stages.

Screens to project films and slides.

Platforms for simultaneous actions.

Movable flats.

Conveyor belts.

Following the example of Soviet proletarian theatre, Piscator puts on plays of political agitation in working-class areas of Berlin. Soon troupes of strolling actor-workers appear all over the city.

The Red Shirts!

The Red Rockets!

The Red Loudspeakers!

It's like a red tide!

Doesn't bother me, I'm colour blind!

Agitprop theatre makes Marxist-Leninist doctrines accessible to a largely illiterate working-class audience.

Brecht remains sceptical about the mass uprisings depicted by Piscator.

That's not going to bring the workers out on to the streets. The seats are too expensive!

Piscator's theatre is revolutionary only in the theatrical sense.

This theatre persists in turning out types that already exist.
Piscator has dealt with the content but not the form.

As far as Brecht is concerned sets are supposed to let the audience know that they are in the theatre rather than in Athens or Venice, for example. The best way to do this is to leave the workings of the set visible.

Neher's sets, for example, ignore perspective.

'If a set doesn't contribute to the production, it detracts from it.'

Caspar Neher,
set designer.

THE THREEPENNY OPERA

Brecht had been thinking for a long time about how to integrate music as an independent element into his plays. Together with **Kurt Weill**, a composer of atonal music, and his collaborator, **Elisabeth Hauptmann**, he undertook an adaptation of *The Beggar's Opera*, written by John Gay in 1728.

Brecht and Weill set to music some ballads by Villon and Kipling.

The first night was in August 1928 at the 'Theat[er
Berliner Ensemble), with sets by Caspar Neher [
Brecht brings the *Beggar's Opera* up to date, se[
Business interests divide Peachum, the boss of [
pimp. Relying on the sex-life and sentimentality [
defenders of the social order and of establishm[e
police ... Conflict breaks out when Macheath d[

BIBLE
PRIVATE
PROPERTY

PEACHUM

BLIND –
from 21.00 h

INSPECTOR
BROWN

hiffbauerdamm' (the favourite venue of the future
Juction by Erich Engel.
n the Victorian London underworld.
rs' agency, from Macheath, a crook and a big-time
Jurgeois world for their profits, the pair become
lity, hence their close collaboration with the
J marry Peachum's daughter, Polly.

POLLY

MACKIE

The marriage scene that Brecht has added to the original takes place in a stable, transformed for the occasion into a glittering reception room. Brown, the police supremo, has been invited.

'This isn't an official visit, Mac.'

'Although our professions keep us on opposite sides of the fence, we've stayed friends through thick and thin.'

Peachum, viewing the departure of his daughter as an irreparable loss for his business, denounces his son-in-law to the police. Though Macheath is on the run, this doesn't stop his regular trips to the brothel. His favourite whore, Jenny, betrays him and Macheath is led off...

… to the gallows!

'What's a skeleton key compared to shares in a company? What's a bank robbery compared with the establishment of a bank? What's killing a man compared with giving him paid work?'

The outcome is completely unexpected – the queen's herald bursts in bearing the royal pardon and a knighthood for Macheath.

You've got to admit that life would be easy if the royal herald always came in the nick of time.

In fact, if the law was always coming down on villains, it would soon lose all credit.

The play was a surprise hit and there were over a thousand performances before it went on a world tour. The songs between the different scenes were on everyone's lips:

1928   Berlin
1929   Zurich and Basle
1930   Vienna
1931   Moscow
1933   New York
1937   Paris

Brecht seeks to reveal the bourgeoisie's affinities with banditry. The bourgeois audience, however, adopts the play and uses it to justify its own hedonism.
Literary history will remember me, he says, if only for having written: 'Food first and morals later.'

In 1927 Brecht and Weill start putting to music the songs of Mahagonny contained in the *Domestic Sermons*, a collection of poetry published the same year. A first dramatization, called *Little Mahagonny*, is presented during the Baden-Baden music festival.

In the final version (*Rise and Fall of the City of Mahagonny*), they call in question the 'culinary' nature of classical opera. Their music, often dissonant and bearing the varied rhythms of jazz and popular song, cannot simply be consumed as it is. It stands in contrast to the scenes, its role being no longer to illustrate sentiments but to interpret the text...

Here too, certain songs caught on.

James Douglas Morrison
rock poet (1943–1971)

MAHAGONNY

The play begins with a parody of the Bible: Fatty, Moses and Begbick (the same character as in *Man equals Man*) are on the run from the police. In the middle of the desert, their van breaks down...

This mini-Las Vegas is to lure into its web the gold won in the West and Alaska. Among the new arrivals, there are four lumberjacks seeking paradise on earth.

Before long, boredom takes over in this city of dreams. Business is going downhill when, faced with the threat of a devastating hurricane (which spares the town at the last moment) the doctrine is proclaimed that 'Everything is permitted'. Henceforth, every kind of crime and debauchery will be allowed in Mahagonny, provided that you can pay! Money is the yardstick of morality and 'the greatest crime that you can commit is not to have enough of it.'

Because he can't pay for a whisky, the lumberjack, Paul Ackermann is sentenced to death.

'Here I sit now and have had just nothing. The joy that I bought was no joy; the freedom they sold me was no freedom.'

'During the last weeks of Mahagonny, the incorrigible survivors demonstrate in the streets for their ideals in an atmosphere of misery and dog-eat-dog.'

Let's keep chaos in our towns!

Liberty for the rich!

Face up to the weak!

DISTRIBUTE WORLDLY GOODS UNJUSTLY!

ALL AGAINST ALL!

With its deliberately simple plot and many allusions, *Mahagonny* brings together theatre for entertainment and theatre with a message.
As it passes through various changes, Mahagonny becomes more and more the symbol of capitalist society, a society plunged into a world economic crisis that has appeared like a hurricane.

1929 – Wall Street Crash

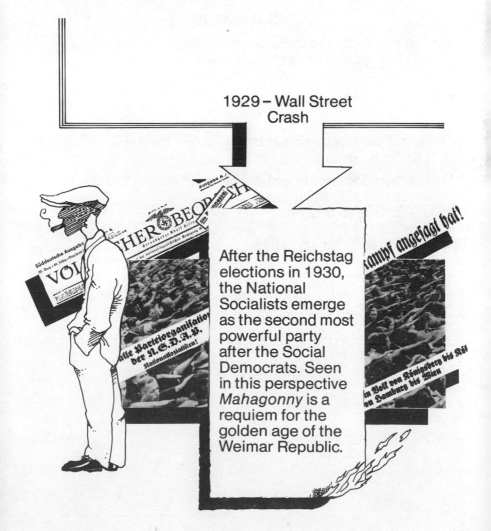

After the Reichstag elections in 1930, the National Socialists emerge as the second most powerful party after the Social Democrats. Seen in this perspective *Mahagonny* is a requiem for the golden age of the Weimar Republic.

Seeing that his plays are misunderstood, and that their success is often due to this misunderstanding, Brecht expresses his political vision of the theatre in comments on *Mahagonny*.
According to him, the dramatic forms on which traditional theatre is based must be introduced into the modern forms of his...

EPIC THEATRE

Here is a short table to indicate the differences in emphasis between the dramatic theatre and the epic theatre:

Dramatic Form of the Theatre

active
involves the spectator in a stage-action
consumes his capacity to act
allows him to have feelings
experience
spectator drawn into something
suggestion
feelings are preserved
the spectator stands inside, experiences with the characters
man is assumed to be known
man unalterable
suspense in awaiting the outcome
one scene exists for another
growth
linear progress
evolutionary inevitability
man as fixed
thought determines Being

Epic Form of the Theatre

narrative
makes the spectator an observer, but
awakens his capacity to act
demands decisions from him
view of the world
he is confronted with something
argument
feelings driven into becoming realisations
the spectator confronts and studies what he sees
man is an object of investigation
man alterable and altering
suspense at the process
each scene for itself
montage
in curves
sudden leaps
man as a process
social Being determines thought

Epic theatre confronts the audience with situations where it must make choices. The spectator can no longer sit passively consuming but has to make decisions for or against what he sees on stage. He becomes productive.

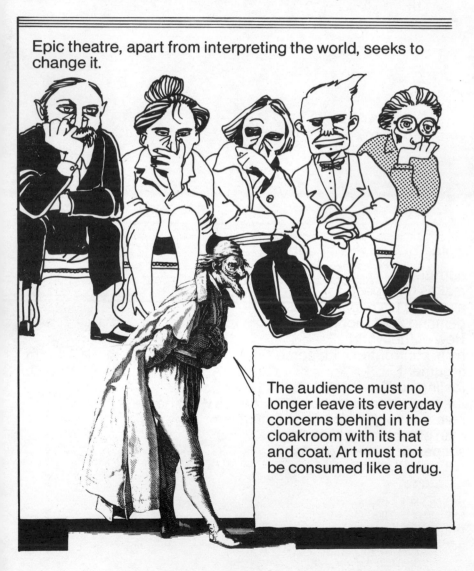

Epic theatre, apart from interpreting the world, seeks to change it.

The audience must no longer leave its everyday concerns behind in the cloakroom with its hat and coat. Art must not be consumed like a drug.

So we get:

At the Dramatic Theatre

At the Epic Theatre

77

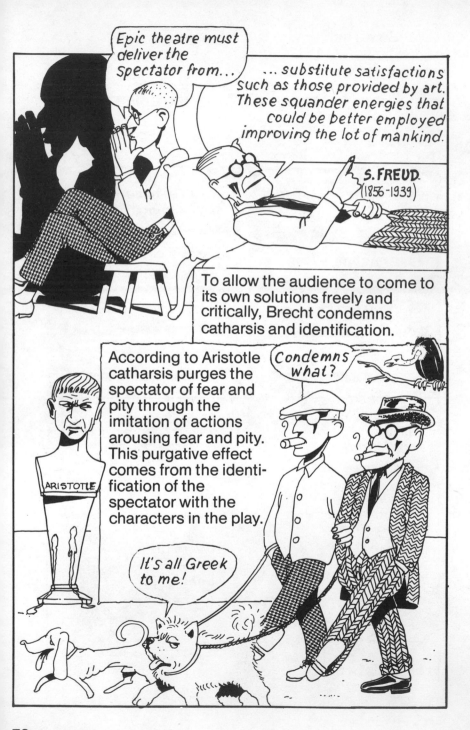

In other words, during a play, the audience tends to identify with the main character. Once this occurs, we share the emotions of fear, pity, etc. experienced by the hero and are, at the same time, psychologically 'purged'. That's what *catharsis* means.

Brecht wants to hear no more of catharsis.

The rejection of catharsis is by no means a rejection of emotion. Brecht merely wants to ensure that emotion does not distract man from realizing his social conscience and taking action.

'Emotions have always had a definite class basis. The form they take is always historical, i.e. specifically tied to a particular period. Emotions are not universal, nor are they outside time.'

AAARGH! Can anyone here feel what I feel?

. . . and indeed, the period is suffering from a severe emotional crisis.

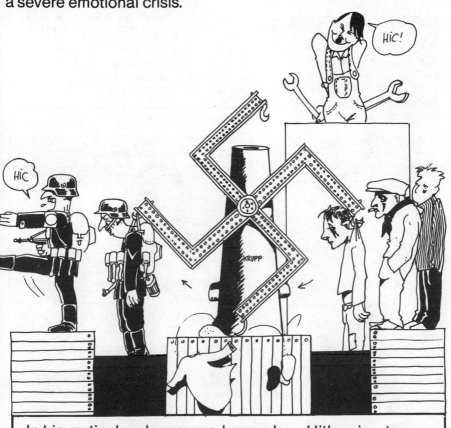

In his meticulously prepared speeches, Hitler aims to use identification to unite the disparate masses under the swastika.

'With regard to the emotions, it is necessary to adopt the same critical attitude as with ideas.'

Brecht finds it impossible to get his epic idea of drama on to the stage of the major theatres where the establishment stands in the way of any fundamental changes.

Ernst v. Wolzogen's
BUNTES THEATER
(Überbrettl)
Gastspiel
vom 18.-31. Januar
BERLINER
SECESSIONSBÜHNE
ALEXANDERSTR. 40.

The establishment will accept what perpetuates the social order and nothing else.

Brecht refuses to conform. The demand for a new type of theatre is, by implication, a demand for a new social order.

It's here that he begins his long, hard road - sometimes pedantic, sometimes clumsy - towards the red dawn of a new society.

Brecht is always ready to use Marxism for the analysis of human relations.

Human destiny is no occult force, it's man himself!

Following his slogan, 'great art always serves great interests',
Brecht develops his didactic theatre to place it at the service
of the revolution.

For what audience however?

Of course, for school children, secular societies, associations and, above all, for the choral societies of the proletariat (14,000 choirs in 1930 with 560,000 members, 70% of them workers).

The didactic play is meant, above all else, to be played. The aim is always to arouse the sense of collectivity among the participants.

Teach through learning.

For the didactic play, the orchestra pit is covered over. The classical stage is transformed into a podium on which the committed members of a collective simulate real-life plots. In Brecht's view, this enables them to work out their ideological position and to be more effective in practice.

Now we don't need an audience

The business of teaching means more to me than any doctrine.'

'The didactic plays are put on especially by small groups (the Young Communists for example...).

The spectator becomes both actor and producer.

That's not going to bring in much!

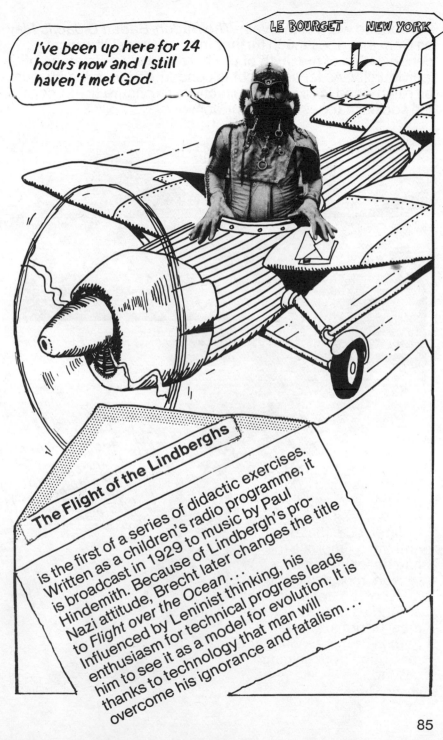

His second work in this vein, *The Baden-Baden Didactic Play on Consent*, goes much further into an almost liturgical denunciation of the myth of the hero, the ultimate stage of individuality. As far as Brecht is concerned individuality must be renounced in favour of collectivity to ensure the success of the social changes that are under way.

The play shows that pity and good-heartedness are isolated acts that do nothing to improve the human lot. For this reason, those who in the midst of the upheavals the around us propose piece-meal reforms, are doing nothing but preventing the revolution from gaining ground.

'Instead of calling for help, abolish violence. Help and violence together form a whole and it is this whole which must be transformed.'

The man in the street tends to think of himself as a complete and independent individual. Yet this individual is everywhere exploited and mutilated like the clown, Mr Schmidt, who appears in the interlude of the play.

HANNS EISLER
composer (1898–1962)

Between 1929 and 1930, Brecht completes the opera for schoolchildren, *He who said yes and he who said no*, and two other political pieces, *The Measures Taken*, and *The Exception and the Rule*, the latter using a chorus. The one point that they all have in common is their location: China, which had been liberated by the nationalist revolution (1925–27).

Brecht's didactic attitude reappears in
1932 in his first (and last) film:

or to whom
does the world
belong?

which he produces in
collaboration with **Slatan
Dudow** and **Hanns Eisler.**
Often censored, it was the
only Communist film to
emerge during the Weimar
Republic.

The film tells the story of a working-class
family living under canvas in a camp on
the outskirts of Berlin: *KUHLE WAMPE.*

Contempt and bloody suppression characterize the attitude of the social-democratic government towards the workers. The principal aim is simple: to bar the way to Communism. This political position will facilitate Hitler's rise to power. The interminable struggles between the Socialists and the Communists will drive many petit-bourgeois and proletarians into the Fascist camp.

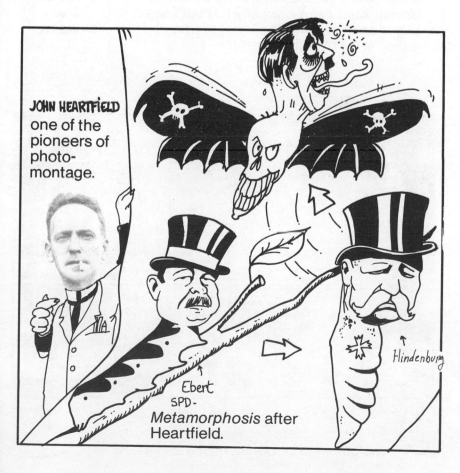

JOHN HEARTFIELD one of the pioneers of photo-montage.

Ebert SPD -
Metamorphosis after Heartfield.

On 1 May 1929 the police force of the social-democratic government puts down worker demonstrations. Brecht witnesses the bloody repression from **Sternberg's** house...

'There were 20 dead in Berlin. Seeing human beings die, Brecht went paler than I have ever known him... This experience was not the least of things which helped to draw him to Communism.'

Since the Russian Revolution the individual is no longer the sole focus of interest.

'We have entered the era of the masses and this fact must be taken into account in the modern drama. It must contain social analysis and directives for action.'

F. STERNBERG

To this end, Brecht has no hesitation is rewriting the texts of certain classics. For example, he lifts some verses from Schiller's *Joan of Arc* to parody humanist idealism in a new play:

Saint Joan of the Stockyards

SCHILLER
(1759–1805)

All right, Bert, I'm ready for the worst.

You know something, Fred, I couldn't keep the whole text.

91

Joan Dark, a Salv[...]
righteousness. Pr[...]
workers' strike to [...]

While working on his didactic plays Brecht carries on his research to get a better understanding of the mechanisms of capitalism. In this play he follows the threads of the world economic crisis of 1929–30.

Speculating on the over-production of meat, Mauler, the king of the Chicago stockyards, drives down prices and wages. While his workers live in total misery, he considers himself a misunderstood philanthropist. For this character, Brecht drawn on J. D. Rockefeller.

! my heart is torn in two:
·cted one way to a noble ideal
·nexplicably also towards profit.

And that's the duality of your capitalist!

starlet, publicly proclaims her
n-violence, she brings the
·re.

Joan comes to realize that Mauler is using her sermons to undermine the workers' claims. She recognizes that no amount of personal integrity is enough to get rid of misery. But as you see:

... She's too late. Her protests are drowned by empty hymns. Having made an exemplary stance and put aside all idealism, Joan has to die to bring the drama to an end.

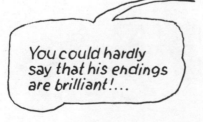

For his first draft of *St Joan*, Brecht wants to know exactly how the Chicago grain market works. As he can't find out from the experts, Brecht plunges into Marx.

It wasn't till I read Das Kapital *that I knew what I'd been writing about.*

With Döblin, he takes courses in political economy at Masch, the Marxist workers' school at Neukölln in Berlin and attends lectures by **Karl Korsch.**

An important Marxist philosopher and Communist deputy who has just been expelled from the Party. His friendship with Brecht will carry on to the end of the book.

Karl **KORSCH**

Brecht is fascinated by the Oriental theatre. He incorporates into his productions the gestures of Japanese Noh theatre.

A further decisive influence is the Moscow theatre of **W. E. Meyerhold,** at the time on tour in Berlin with a play by **S. Tretiakov.**

Fantastic! Your actors know how to act with their heads and their hearts at the same time!

'My actors learned first of all how to think, and then how to think materialistically.'

They are brought together by Walter Benjamin.

TRETIAKOV

MEYERHOLD

Meyerhold had develcped a system of physical training called Biomechanics to rationalize body movement on stage.

His actors speak directly to the audience to put over their revolutionary message.

Brecht, inspired by their systematic use of gesture and ritual in expression, borrows from them what he calls: the **social gestus**.

The social gestus is the sum of all the gestures, facial expressions and declarations of attitude of an individual or a group towards others.

and what might that mean?

Examples! Give me examples! I can't bear it when I don't understand!!

Lovely piece of mullet... fine, fresh mullet!

All right then, for example: Someone selling a fish displays the gestus of selling... A policeman beating up a prisoner... A man writing his will... There's always a social gestus.

THE MOTHER

In memory of Rosa Luxemburg, Brecht adapts *The Mother*, a novel written by Gorky in exile in 1907.
Following the execution of her revolutionary son Pavel, Pelagea Vlassova is gradually won over to the Russian Revolution, and becomes one of its leading figures.

The Mother has its première on the anniversary of the assassination of Rosa Luxemburg. The performances are under continual police surveillance. One evening, Helene Weigel, playing the Mother, is arrested right in the middle of the play...

The political situation gets so dangerous that theatres no longer dare to put on his plays...
Actor-workers take over the task until...

... on 27 February 1933 ... the Reichstag is burned down.
On 28 February the decree is passed which allows Hitler to
get rid of parliamentary and all other forms of opposition.
The same day Bert and his family leave a country in which the
word 'proletariat' can no longer be uttered.

ACT 3 : Exile

Hairy, unshaven, smelling as strong as a soldier emerging from the trenches, this young man is Bertolt Brecht starting out on an exile that is to last for fifteen years.

With the help of Danish friends, Brecht and his family settle down in Denmark. This enables him to stay in contact with his homeland and with the growing numbers of exiles who find themselves hospitably received in Denmark.
Soon afterwards, Brecht buys a house in Skovbostrand.

Like many other emigrés, Brecht hopes to return to Germany before long. Meanwhile, where to stay? Finally, after Prague, Vienna and Zurich, he settles on Paris – but only for a few days.

His ballet, *The Seven Deadly Sins of the Petit-Bourgeois*, set to music by Kurt Weill, is put on at the Champs-Elysées theatre.

These sins are an invention of the dominant class to distract the people from the wretchedness of their lives.

Asceticism! Chastity! A curse on the enjoyment of the senses!

What a joker! These are the real virtues!

In Paris, he comes in contact again with his young collaborator, **Margarete Steffin**. The two of them go off to visit Feuchtwanger who, like Stefan Zweig and Thomas Mann, has taken refuge at Sanary-sur-mer, a health resort favoured by the best German writers.

The Threepenny Novel

In this expanded version of the *Threepenny Opera*, the gangster Macheath has become a banker – true to his own motto: what is robbing a bank compared to establishing one? This Swiftian satire on the capitalist system reads like a detective story. Published in Amsterdam in 1934, it is rejected by his Communist Party colleagues who feel that the writing is not sufficiently realist.

In his thatched cottage in Denmark, Brecht gets down to work again on his play, *Round Heads and Pointed Heads*. It had been published but was seized from the press by the Nazis...

The advance of Nazism forces him to review his interpretation of Fascist ideology – especially after the proclamation of the Nuremberg Laws on race in 1935:

Round Heads and, POINTED HEADS

The inspiration for this parable was *Measure for Measure*, considered by Brecht to be the most 'progressive' of Shakespeare's plays.

The Kingdom of Yahoo, an imaginary country borrowed from Swift, is shaken by a peasants' revolt sparked off by their inability to pay their rents.

To head off a revolution organized by the Sickle League, the financial aristocracy promotes Iberin, a demagogue who has invented a new racist theory.

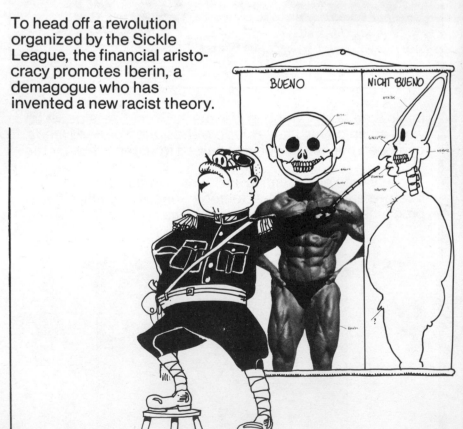

Iberin uses this theory to obscure the difference between rich and poor by dividing people into good (Round Heads) and bad (Pointed Heads).
Declaring that the Pointed Heads are responsible for all the ills of the country, he succeeds in dividing and weakening the insurgents and in re-establishing the power of the old landowners, just as had happened in Germany.

Oh! We've had masters enough
We've had tigers and then hyenas
We've had eagles and then pigs.
But whatever they are, they need feeding.
Some, it's said, are less bad than others
But a boot's a boot
When it's walking over you.
We don't need any new masters
No, we can really
do without them.

It is in talking of *Round Heads and Pointed Heads* that Brecht for the first time uses the term **verfremdungseffekt** (distancing effect).

The purpose is to stop the spectator being spellbound by the actors and to let him maintain a critical distance.

Whereas identification reduces extraordinary events to the level of the commonplace, distancing makes common-place events rare and astonishing.

What is known, because it is known, is unknown.

HEGEL
1770 - 1831
PHILOSOPHER

(This play is the last in the didactic cycle.)
To remind you of the story in Livy:
Three warriors of the Horatii face three of the Curiatii who are more heavily armed.

Two of the Horatii fall. The third, pretending to run away, succeeds in separating his pursuers and kills them one by one.

Brecht is putting forward a strategy for anti-Fascist resistance.

During the first years of his exile, Brecht makes a number of 'business' trips to London, New York, Paris and Moscow, the outposts of the German emigré community. He wants to set up a German theatre in the USSR but it is quickly brought home to him that his presence is undesirable – the Stalinist vice is already tightening on the revolution and its children. Friends like **Carola Neher** and **Tretiakov** will not return from Stalin's gulags.

Brecht's encounter with Chinese theatre in the USSR reinforces his intention to use ancient techniques of distancing.

A chinese artist doesn't act as if, apart from the walls surrounding him on three sides, there were also a fourth. He doesn't hide the fact that he knows he is being watched. Thus the illusion maintained on the European stage is removed. The spectator can no longer imagine himself an invisible witness to real events.
The artist observes himself.

'The Chinese actor is never in a trance. If he is interrupted, he doesn't have to put aside his role. Once the interruption is over, he starts again exactly where he left off. When he goes on stage, he is already fully into his character and he doesn't mind if scenes are shifted while he is acting.'

Mei Ian Fan, a Chinese actor seen in Moscow in 1935, inspires him to write a number of articles on the effects of distancing.

With the actor distancing himself from his character, the spectator is prevented from identifying with him.

Brecht insists that his actors must not enter body and soul into their parts. He wants the spectator to realize that he is in the theatre and not somewhere else.

The epic actor dissects his part, exposing all the contradictions in the character.

Just like the Chinese actor who can break off and then
return to the exact point in his part, the epic actor can
stand back in the middle of the play to recapitulate or give
his opinion
and thus
provide an
overview
for the
spectator.

In interpreting a role, the
actor gives his point of
view.

Brecht's ideas on distancing are vehemently criticized by the proponents of socialist realism in Moscow. The Hungarian theoretician Georg Lukács, in particular judges the epic theatre to be an aberration of the avant-garde.

G.Lukacs
(1885–1971)

Let's get rid of bourgeois decadence with its Joyces and Kafkas!! We need more Sholokhovs.

But Kafka is the only truly Bolshevik writer!

How Kafkaesque!

117

In June 1935 the International Congress of Writers for the Defence of Culture takes place at the Mutualité in Paris. The writers of 37 countries come together to form a united front against Fascism.

Among the German intellectuals:

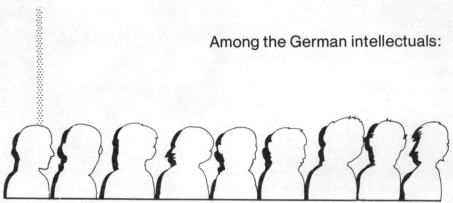

Heinrich Mann☞ Alfred Döblin ☞ L. Feuchtwanger ☞ Max Brod ☞ Egon E. Kisch ☞ Ernst Bloch ☞ W. Benjamin ☞ J-R. Becher ☞ Anna Seghers

Political differences, however, prevent any common action.

Founder of the German library of burned books.

Every German exile wants his own political tendency

Bah! Come and let off steam at Meudon!

JEAN RENOIR, whose films Brecht enjoys as much as his cooking.

In July 1936 the Fascist generals
under Franco rebel against the
elected Republican government.

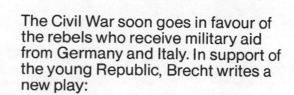

The Civil War soon goes in favour of
the rebels who receive military aid
from Germany and Italy. In support of
the young Republic, Brecht writes a
new play:

On 26 April 1937, the
German air force
bombs the town of
Guernica. Toll: 2,500
dead and injured.

In this play Brecht attacks the neutralist policy of the 'Western democracies', and particularly that of the Popular Front, in face of German and Italian interventionism. Spain is the training ground on which the Fascists prepare their armies for the coming World War.

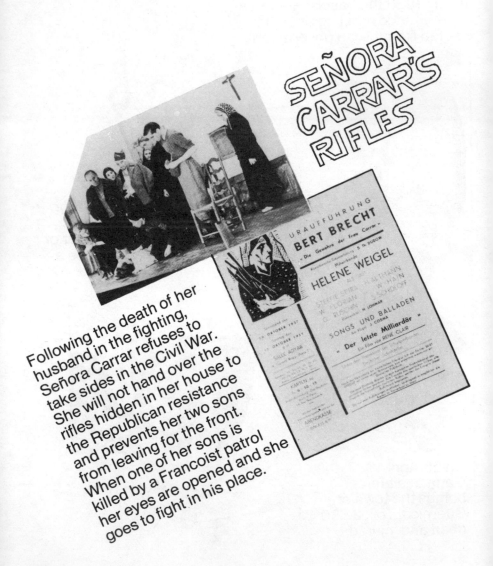

SEÑORA CARRAR'S RIFLES

Following the death of her husband in the fighting, Señora Carrar refuses to take sides in the Civil War. She will not hand over the rifles hidden in her house to the Republican resistance and prevents her two sons from leaving for the front. When one of her sons is killed by a Francoist patrol her eyes are opened and she goes to fight in his place.

For this very short play, Brecht abandons certain epic elements:

'To make our anti-Fascist propaganda more effective, sometimes it's necessary to fight them with their own weapons.'

The play is performed in Paris while the battle goes on in Madrid, where the inhabitants and the remnants of the International Brigades are being killed.

The defeat of democratic Spain in 1939 is only the prelude to the defeat of France shortly afterwards.

Another première takes place not much later. It is that of the play:

Fear and Misery of the Third Reich

which uses eye-witness accounts and news items to depict Germany from 1933 to 1938 with all its mechanisms of routine intimidation, denunciation and corruption – and alongside it, a growing resistance.

This montage of 24 scenes covers every social circle and with it, Brecht contradicts the popular view that Fascism is the work merely of a few 'demonic' individuals. It is only the opportunism or resignation of those who want to save their skins that perpetuates the system.
In this totalitarian world, there's but one short step between being turned in and being strung up.

This time, war is the solution to the problem created by Germany arriving too late to be included in the imperialist division of world markets.

Danish friends help Brecht to make a clandestine crossing into neutral Sweden.

How much room do you need?

Enough for three women, two children and me.

'Writers today can't write quickly enough to keep up with the politicians who declare war.'

For their war propaganda, the Nazis popularize a new medium: radio.

But how to counter this litany of lies?

Brecht, whose writings no longer reach his fellow countrymen in Germany, prepares a pacifist play, *The Trial of Lucullus*, for Swedish radio. Sweden, however, obliged to remain neutral towards its belligerent neighbour, doesn't dare to broadcast it.

In the end, the play is reworked as an opera and set to music by

PAUL DESSAU

In the kingdom of the dead, General Lucullus (106–107 BC) who brought several areas of Asia Minor into the Roman Empire, is waiting to find out whether he will be cast down into Hades or whether he will live in the Elysian Fields.

A tribunal of ghosts (who in life had been men of the people) hears the witnesses one by one in order to judge the 'benefits' of his expeditions.

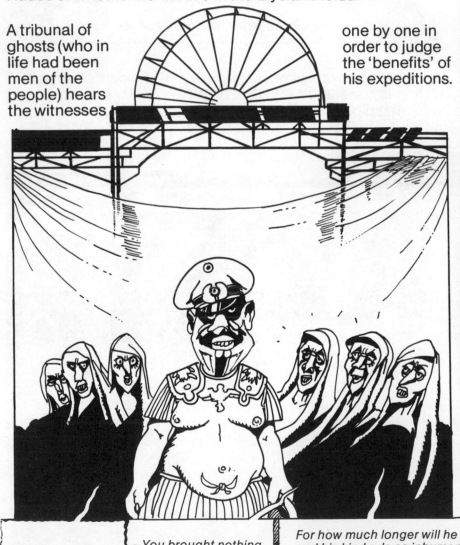

80,000 soldiers to enrich Rome – but who is Rome?

You brought nothing back for us but you always took our children for your legions.

For how much longer will he and his kind rule as inhuman masters over manking? So, let him go down into nothingness! Him and all those like him!

It is shown that his supposedly glorious deeds are founded on the endless suffering of subject peoples... We learn that such heroes always serve the particular interests of the dominant class which then describes their crimes as glories. What we learn from our history books about their greatness is worthy of anything but admiration.

'Who built Thebes of the seven gates?
Books give us the names of kings.
Was it kings that dragged the blocks of stone?
The young Alexander conquered India. On his own?
Caesar conquered the Gauls.
Did he march without even a cook?
When the Armada went down, Philip of Spain wept.
No one else wept?
Every ten years, a great man.
And the cost, who was it that paid?
For every tale, the same questions.'

                                                    B.B.

'Questions put by a worker who reads.'

Brecht measures the deeds of political leaders in terms of the general good: what did the people gain from them? In fact, these political criminals are often called 'great' because they have committed great crimes.

Of all the mother roles created by Brecht, the character of Mother Courage remains the best known and at the same time, the most contradictory. Unlike Pelagea Vlassova (*the Mother*) and Señora Carrar, Mother Courage never becomes a revolutionary. She remains incorrigible and believes in war to the very end.

She too realizes that war is the continuation of business by other means.

Owner of a canteen wagon during the Thirty Years War (1618–1648) Mother Courage, with her three children, follows the armies that confront each other across a devastated Europe ... War is her livelihood.

'But what is war but private trading That deals in blood instead of boots?'

Realizing that victory as much as defeat is always at the expense of the lower classes, Courage hopes to profit from the war without paying her dues.

Wrong! She pays with the lives of her children without drawing any conclusion from it.

Why is it that Mother Courage never learns?

She learns as little from the catastrophe as the guinea-pig does from biology.

'Misfortune in itself is a poor teacher. Its pupils learn hunger and thirst, but seldom hunger for truth or thirst for knowledge.

In wartime, virtues become crimes. Religion and honour are used just to camouflage the true purpose of the war which is to maintain at all costs the exploitation of the people by the aristocracy and the church...

'One sermon of mine can put a regiment in such a frame of mind that it'll treat the enemy like a flock of sheep.'

'For virtues aren't their own reward, only wickednesses are, that's how the world goes and it didn't ought to.'

... but the première of the play is postponed until 1949.

The Good Person of Szechwan

In this parable completed in 1941, Brecht poses the question: How far is it possible for a man to live in degrading conditions and yet remain good?

Three gods descend to earth and scour China in search of a good person. In the capital of Szechwan, they are shown the door just about everywhere. Only the prostitute, Shen Teh, agrees to take them in.

When they leave, the gods give her some money for her trouble. She uses it to buy a tobacco shop and decides to go in for good works. Immediately, however, she is beset by swarms of beggars and parasites. Overwhelmed, Shen-Teh has to invent a ruthless cousin for herself who can save the business by applying the cruel laws of the market.

So, is man good or bad?

If the circumstances prevent it, there is no way that we can be good. Let's start by improving conditions. Forget morality that can't be applied.

The gods are no great help either.

'What a world we have found here! Nothing but poverty, debasement and dilapidation. Even the landscape crumbles away before our eyes. Beautiful trees are lopped off by cables and over the mountains we see great clouds of smoke and hear the thunder of guns, and nowhere a good person who survives it!'

'People have enough to do saving their skin. Good intentions lead them to the brink of the abyss and good deeds push them over.'

So what's the conclusion?

Dear audience, find the missing end! There must be one! There must!

Why does Brecht so often speak in parables?

Through the parable, Brecht is able to explain in a simple way the complex phenomena of our society such as war, religion, inflation, racism and so on... For him, it's not enough to give naturalist representations; he has to show the underlying mechanisms.

Experimental theatre!! Frightful!!

This is scientific theatre. We follow well-defined models and methods to make the mechanisms of social life comprehensible. Man is a variable of his environment and the environment is a variable of man. The potential for change is enormous!

Education through entertainment, right?!

In April 1940, with the entry of German troops in hasty retreat to Finland. The economic situation is undernourished. The Brechts, waiting for the Wuolijoki, to her estate at Marlebäk.

136

137

Ruth Berlau rejoins them. Apart from the odd family row, this intimate circle enables him to continue working even in exile.

RUTH BERLAU —   B.B – HELENE WEIGEL – MARGERETE STEFFIN

The German army is always at their heels. Brecht follows its deadly progress on the radio:

'I listen to the messages of victory from the very dregs
   of society.
With curiosity, I examine the map of the continent.
Right at the top, in Lapland,
On the icy Arctic sea
I see a tiny opening.'

B.B.

Hella Wuolijoki (1886–1954) is a tremendous storyteller of popular Finnish tales...

Inspired by one of her stories, and by the Finnish landscape, Brecht begins his popular play: *Mr Puntila and His Man Matti*...

Puntila, a landowner and heavy drinker, has a split personality. When he's drunk, he gets very matey with his workers and talks almost like a socialist to soothe his guilty conscience. The next day, however, when the drink has worn off, he regrets his promises and returns to his old vindictive, misogynist self (as his position requires). Then he takes it out on his whipping-boy Matti.

You won't get me drinking again, you little shit! You wouldn't lift your little finger except to save yourself from starvation, you parasite...

Yes, Mr Puntila.

Matti, you're my friend, my guide on the long, hard road. I get a thirst just looking at you. How much do I give you a month?

300 marks a month, sir.

I'm raising it to 350 because I'm so pleased with you.

kind of
his? I
hing but
t people
orning
t and
ut the
hay...

loot,
e
unists
's
a's
e
u!

141

Matti realizes that this dual personality enables Puntila to exploit others all the more.

'It's time for valets to turn their back on you. There'll be no such thing as a good master until everyone's his own.'

This split personality – in Puntila as in Mauler of *St Joan of the Stockyards* – is shared by all those in positions of power. Hence their morality is also dual: they feel a temporary need to act well in order to compensate for all their dirty business.

HEGEL

It is this ambivalent relationship between master and servant that weighs so heavily.

No valets – no more masters!

1.7.1940

The world is changing by the hour. It seems to me that a growing number of things have been disappearing but there was always the radio. Then one day, Vienna went off the air. Then Prague. So for a while we listened to Warsaw. Then Warsaw went dead. Copenhagen and Oslo began broadcasting only in German. Now, Paris has gone. Of all the Western democracies, only London remains. For how long?

'Workbook'

Deutsche Baumeister

16.9.1940

It would be incredibly difficult to describe my state of mind when, having followed the Battle of Britain on the radio and in the mediocre Finno-Swedish press, I wrote Puntila – Puntila means next to nothing to me, the war everything. I can write everything about Puntila, nothing about the war.

'Workbook'

In 1940 Brecht writes *Emigré Conversations*, influenced by his reading of *Jacques le Fataliste*.
Two German refugees, the Jewish scientist Ziffel and the worker Kalle, meet at the station in Helsinki which is crawling with Nazi agents. In low voices, they analyse the roots of Nazism and its associated phenomena: spirit of order and concentration camps, racial theories and nationalism, conquest of raw materials through war...

As for passports, they were invented above all in the interests of order... without them, we'd be untraceable when the time came for our deportation... it would be total anarchy...

The idea of race is the petit-bourgeois way of getting into the nobility. In himself, the petit-bourgeois is no more imperialist than the aristocrat. Why should he be? It's only that he has a worse conscience and needs a pretext for his expansion...

The problem for the Germans is how to make enough masters. Once, in the concentration camp, the commandant bawled us out: 'How can such weaklings and pacifists as you expect to dominate the world?'

A German invasion growing daily more likely, the Brechts await their US visas with impatience. Meanwhile, Bert sketches out a play for the American theatre...

Here we are again in Chicago... A dark cloud of crisis...
profit... and corruption hangs over the town.

Brecht continues his demystification of great historical
characters with his comedy:
THE RESISTIBLE RISE OF ARTURO UI

Arturo Ui (alias Hitler) and his gang are totally bankrupt, morally and financially. As the economic crisis deepens, he has to muscle in on the Chicago cauliflower cartel. In his rise to power, he employs the same methods as Hitler: words and weapons!

Dogsborough (alias Hindenburg), involved in a corruption scandal, gets caught up with financial dealers. The financiers make use of his prestige with the masses to legitimize their own monopoly of power.

Arturo Ui crawls to Dogsborough to get himself accepted as his legal successor and manages to do so just in time. Suddenly, this Al Capone has become a reputable businessman, respected even by his adversaries.

For Brecht, Nazism is not the opposite of democracy but a distortion of it in time of crisis.

147

As in *St Joan of the Stockyards*, Brecht uses classical verse as a distancing technique. The rhetoric of Arturo Ui and his gang is a parody of the empty, solemn speeches of the Nazis. Behind the pretty words lies a bloody reality.

Believe me! You must believe that I seek only what is best for you and that I know what is best!

Death is a good customer.

Brecht reveals the theatrical nature of Fascism. As with the idealistic rhetoric of Arturo Ui, passing off the crimes of his gang, so Hitler's speeches appeal to the instincts of the masses and prepare them for genocide.

'The gas chambers of the IG Farben Trust are a monument to the bourgeois culture of these decades.'

'Workbook' 13.4.1948

At the end of July the Brechts leave for California. Brec
well-loved collaborator, Margarete Steffin, who dies of

There is more sad news in store: his close friend, Walter
Benjamin, has committed suicide just short of the Spanish
frontier while fleeing from the Nazi plague.

to leave behind his
...ulosis in Moscow.

'I have lost my guide as I enter the wilderness.'

Brecht and his family settle down in Santa Monica, near Hollywood, where there is already a whole colony of German exiles (Heinrich and Thomas Mann, Fritz Lang, Döblin, and Feuchtwanger, who has escaped from a concentration camp in France).

'Everything here is for sale, from a shrug of the shoulders
to an idea. That's the custom. You've got to think
constantly of the client so that you're all the time either a
buyer or a seller. I think they would even sell their piss in
a urinal…'

'Workbook' 21.1.1942

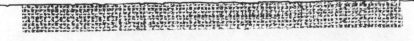

In order to make a stand with regard to events in Europe,
Brecht drafts two more plays:

The Visions of SIMONE MACHARD

A girl of thirteen sees her village occupied by the Nazis. Disgusted by the collaboration of the village notables and inspired by the example of St Joan of Arc, she sets fire to the fuel dump that has fallen into the hands of the enemy.

'After the conqueror occupies your town he must feel he's isolated, on his own. No one of you must ever permit him to come in. He can't count as a guest, so treat him like vermin.'

'They are coming! At their head is the drummer with a voice like a wolf and a drum stretched with a Jew's skin.'

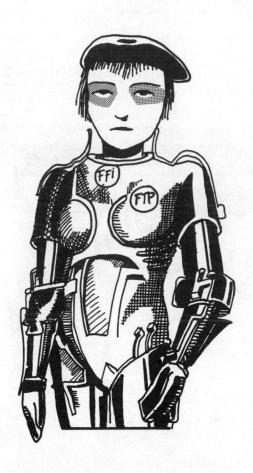

Brecht fades in and out a series of real
and imaginary scenes. In her visions
Simone retraces the martyrdom of the
saint and foretells her own fate.
Betrayed by the collaborators, she is put
away in a psychiatric hospital. Her
actions, however, stir up a patriotic
resistance movement.

In the winter of 1941–42, the Red Army, at the cost of fearful losses, succeeds in halting the German invasion at Stalingrad. This is the turning point of the war. The retreating Nazis put down all disobedience in the occupied territories.

For the occasion, Brecht revives Hašek's novel *The Good Soldier Schweyk*, which he had already adapted for the stage with Piscator. It now becomes:

SCHWEYK IN THE SECOND WORLD WAR.

As Marshal Goering put it: 'The Führer cannot always be understood immediately, he's too great... He wanted to put up a building to stretch from Leipzig to Dresden, a temple in memory of Germany once it's gone under.

Hitler's a wet fart, I'm telling you because you're drunk. And who's responsible for Hitler? Them that handed him Czechoslovakia on a plate at Munich for 'peace in our time', and a fat long time it was too.
But the war's lasted all right, and for a lot of people it's been 'war in our time' from what I can see.

FRITZ LANG.
(1890–1976)
film-maker.

Brecht feels less at home in California than anywhere else. Hollywood has no interest in his plays so Brecht has to grub about for small commissions. To make ends meet, he collaborates with Fritz Lang on a film about the Czech resistance fighting the Hazi butcher, Heydrich. It is called *Hangmen Also Die*. Flavoured with Hollywood sauce, the film becomes a sentimental fresco filled with every kind of unlikely occurrence. After the film, Brecht and Lang fall out. This is the only one of fifty scripts suggested by Brecht that gets produced.

After the film, Brecht and Lang fall out. This is the only one of fifty scenarios suggested by Brecht that gets produced.

Aeurk!!

The members of the Frankfurt Sociology Institute (1923–50) are also in exile in Hollywood. Brecht cannot avoid them.

The Frankfurt Institute is a goldmine of ideas for the 'Tui' novel.

In this fragmentary novel the Tuis (*Tellecktuals-in*) are venal intellectuals, knowledge merchants who do not put their brains to any practical political work.

As the German army retreats, Brecht is already hoping for a post-war socialist Germany. It is in this perspective that we must see:

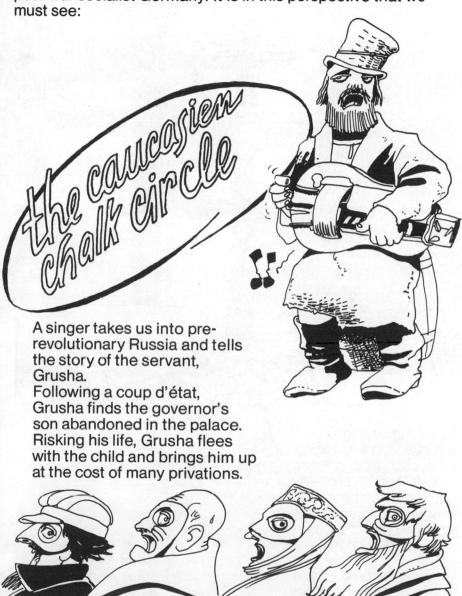

the caucasien chalk circle

A singer takes us into pre-revolutionary Russia and tells the story of the servant, Grusha.
Following a coup d'état, Grusha finds the governor's son abandoned in the palace. Risking his life, Grusha flees with the child and brings him up at the cost of many privations.

The very antithesis of his heroines is the archetypal 'couldn't-care-less character' Schweyk.

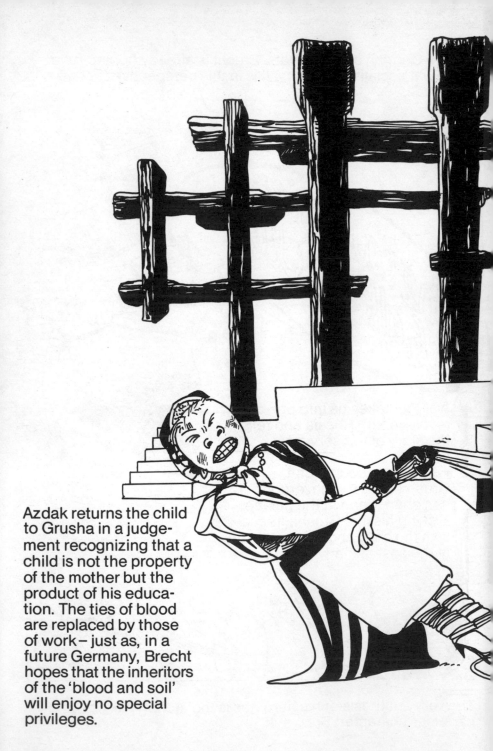

Azdak returns the child to Grusha in a judgement recognizing that a child is not the property of the mother but the product of his education. The ties of blood are replaced by those of work – just as, in a future Germany, Brecht hopes that the inheritors of the 'blood and soil' will enjoy no special privileges.

Many years later, the governor's wife demands the return of the child to get her hands on his inheritance. Azdak, who in the political upheavals of the times has been pitchforked into the position of judge, must now decide the question. His judgments become increasingly liberal, and by altering the current laws in force he rules in favour of the poor. Like Solomon, he puts the mothers to the test: whoever gets the child out of the circle is the true mother.

Between 1943 and 1947, Brecht makes several trips to New York to keep up contact with German refugee circles (Dessau, Weill, Grosz, Piscator, etc.) and to get one of his plays performed on Broadway. But his work is considered too political and not commercial enough.

Brecht consoles himself by rewriting the *Manifesto of the Communist Party* in verse – another unfinished project.

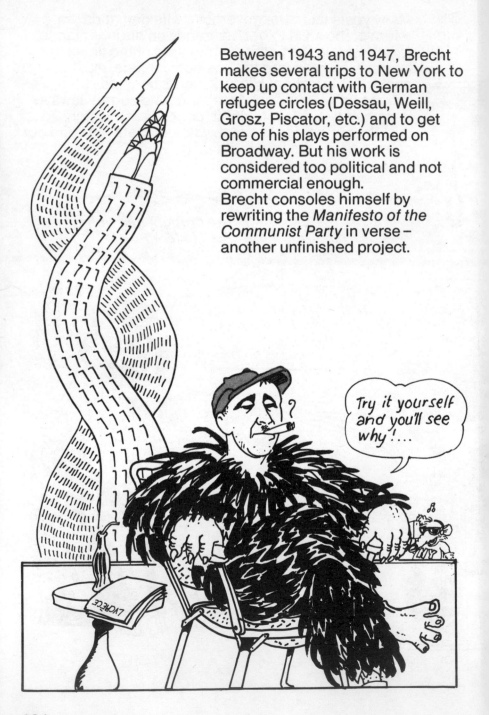

Try it yourself and you'll see why! ....

Brecht makes his last attempt to interest American producers with *The Caucasian Chalk Circle*, an adaptation of a 13th century Chinese play.

Hitler's armies have already surrendered and the war in the Pacific against the Japanese has almost been won when, in August 1945, the US air force drops atomic bombs on Hiroshima and Nagasaki.

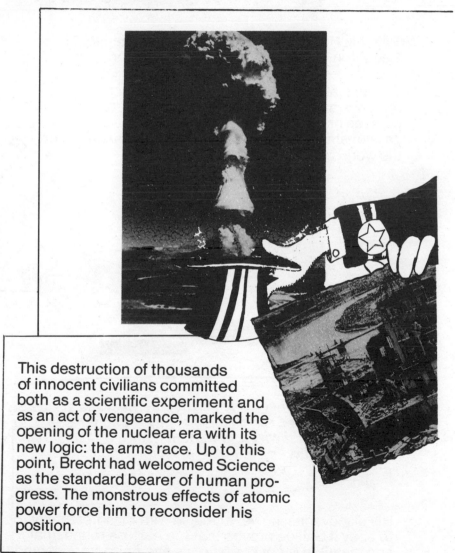

This destruction of thousands of innocent civilians committed both as a scientific experiment and as an act of vengeance, marked the opening of the nuclear era with its new logic: the arms race. Up to this point, Brecht had welcomed Science as the standard bearer of human progress. The monstrous effects of atomic power force him to reconsider his position.

Brecht takes the opportunity to bring out a manuscript saved from the days of his exile in Scandinavia.

The Life of Galileo

With his Hollywood neighbour, actor Charles Laughton, he makes an American version.

Galileo Galilei (1564–1642) lives in Venice and in Florence at the court of the Medicis where he pursues his scientific research. He believes passionately that science and human reason will rid the world of misery and superstition.

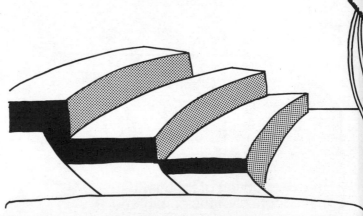

'It has been shown that the heavens are empty... And the earth rolls happily round the sun... and the fishwives, merchants, princes and cardinals, and even the Pope, roll with it.'

His discoveries, however, clash with the interests of the Ch
to obey if Galileo proves that the earth is round, that it's no
and that God is not keeping his eye on us from behind the

r all, who's going
e of the universe

When Galileo brings out his studies in Italian and not in Latin – so that everyone will be able to understand them – he is summoned before the court of the Inquisition.

He is forced to retract.

Ouch!

Attached to his comfortable life, he opts for internal exile and carries on his research secretly.

Hee, hee!

'I hold that the sole aim of Science is to reduce the miseries of human life. If men of science, intimidated by selfish masters, are satisfied with accumulating knowledge for knowledge's sake, Science itself may fall sick.'

and today?

What did the President want to see you about, dear colleague?...

about my new anti-Communist gas... What about you?

Oh! About my new system for purifying the minds of our good new American citizens.'

Following the death of President Roosevelt, Truman's government is marked by its anti-Communism. The 'Committee of Enquiry on Un-American Activities' is established in Hollywood and Brecht, like a good number of other artists denounced by colleagues, is summoned before it.

Mr Brecht, are you a member of the Communist Party?

Do you remember anyone ever asking you to become a member of the Communist Party?

He's putting on a good show.

Er, no, no, well I mean... No, I don't think so, maybe, I can't remember...

ACT 4: Return

The day after his cross-examination, Brecht takes the plane for Zurich. The next few months are spent in Switzerland where he meets up again with his old friend Neher. Together, they prepare an adaptation of Sophocles's *Antigone* (with Helene Weigel in the title role).

Brecht follows developments in Germany with caution. Before committing himself to stay there, he obtains an Austrian passport so that he can leave at any time. Arriving in East Berlin in October 1948, he is dismayed to find the starving survivors wandering among the ruins and bomb craters.

'Berlin, an etching by Churchill, after an idea by Hitler. Berlin, mountains of debris around Potsdam look down on totally deserted streets while the airlift transport planes drone through the night sky.'

'Workbook'
27.10.1948

In the winter, Soviet troops block access to West Berlin to prevent a West German state from being set up under the aegis of the Western powers. The Americans provide an airlift that supplies the beleaguered population for months.

Brecht sees the collapse of his dream of a reunified socialist Germany with an international theatre centre.

The chips are down: in May 1949, the Federal Republic is proclaimed in the west, followed five months later by the Democratic Republic in the east – two buffer states for future confrontations of the superpowers.

Brecht observes a new misery in Germany:

... *nothing is settled and nearly everything is already bungled.*

Having refrained from doing so for 15 years, Brecht puts on *Mother Courage* to music by Paul Dessau.

PAUL DESSAU
composer.

Brecht thinks the play is more relevant than ever, as the majority seem to have learned as little from the war as Mother Courage herself. The lukewarm official response confirms his view. The work is thought to be too pacifist for the falling temperatures of the Cold War.

Brecht's next play is the profession of his faith in Communism.

Convinced of their ability to establish socialism in a democratic way, the Communards fail. They guarantee the liberties and property of a bourgeoisie which reciprocates by joining ranks with the enemy and massacring them. In showing the defeat of the Commune, Brecht concludes that the temporary suspension of individual rights is necessary for the construction of socialism.

THE DAYS OF THE COMMUNE

It lights the way to the dictatorship of the proletariat.

Such demands are further to the left than the party is prepared to allow. It is feared that, so soon after the Nazi dictatorship, the idea might stir up the population.

Solidarnosc

Similarly, his *Short Organum* for the theatre (written in 1948) arouses a lively controversy. Brecht stresses the experimental and sensual nature of his drama and calls on the scientific empiricism of Francis Bacon (1561–1626). He looks forward to a time when the act of learning will once more be an act of joy.

'The theatre needs no justification other than entertainment, but this it requires absolutely.
The theatre can provide weaker (simple) and stronger (complex) pleasures. The latter, to be found in great dramatic works, reach their climax just as the sexual act reaches it in love; they are more ramified, richer in mediation, more contradictory and richer in consequences... The theatre must surprise its audience and this is done by the technique of distancing it from what is familiar. Such a technique enables the theatre to exploit dialectical materialism, in which things exist only in so far as they are being transformed and are thus not in harmony with themselves. This applies equally to the feelings, attitudes and opinions through which the social life of man is expressed.'
After this important manifesto, Brecht is often to speak of his dialectic theatre.

Only that which is filled with contradictions is alive!

His dialectical concept of the theatre derives from the reading of a pamphlet by Mao Tse-tung entitled: 'On Contradiction'. Contradictions and conflicts between old and new are seen to be necessary and inevitable for the development of socialism.

Revolutionary China seems to Brecht to offer a ray of hope whereas in the GDR contradictions are building up. Economic stagnation and ideological hardening lead to an acceleration in emigration.

176

After long negotiations, Brecht and Weigel succeed in getting permission to form their own troupe: **The Berliner Ensemble**. Under difficult conditions they recruit a new generation of actors and playwrights.

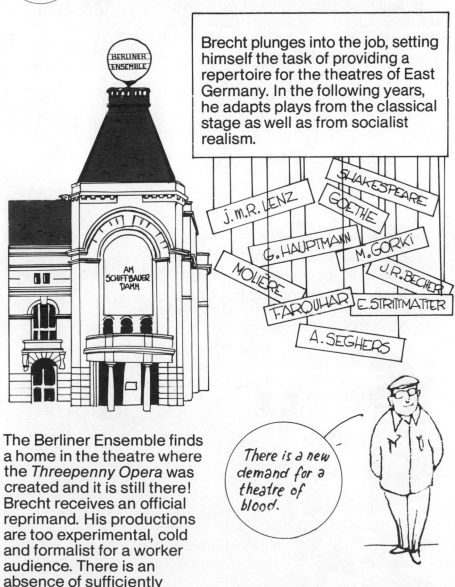

Brecht plunges into the job, setting himself the task of providing a repertoire for the theatres of East Germany. In the following years, he adapts plays from the classical stage as well as from socialist realism.

SHAKESPEARE

J. M. R. LENZ

GOETHE

G. HAUPTMANN

M. GORKI

MOLIÈRE

J. R. BECHER

FARQUHAR

E. STRITTMATTER

A. SEGHERS

AM SCHIFFBAUER DAMM

The Berliner Ensemble finds a home in the theatre where the *Threepenny Opera* was created and it is still there! Brecht receives an official reprimand. His productions are too experimental, cold and formalist for a worker audience. There is an absence of sufficiently positive emotions.

There is a new demand for a theatre of blood.

His work deviates from the theories of the Russian producer, K. S. Stanislavski, which have now become the official doctrine of social realist theatre. For this theatre the actor requires intimately lived experience of his role which he enters into in an almost trance-like state.

Sentimental acrobatics!

Brecht detests the short-circuiting of consciousness.

Lets have emotions which do not exclude reason!

A large-scale conference on the Stanislavski method is organized, challenging epic theatre. Brecht plays down the conflict.

Even Stanislavski used distancing - though, of course, he wasn't aware of it!

... but their methods remain incompatible.

Konstantin Sergeievitch STANISLAVSKI 1863 - 1938

In June 1953, just after the death of Stalin, the workers of East Berlin demonstrate against new working conditions. The revolt, which quickly reaches other towns, is put down by Soviet tanks.

'After the 17 June uprising, the secretary of the Union of Writers has leaflets distributed in the Stalinallee. The people, says the leaflet, have, through their own fault, lost the confidence of the government. They will have to pull up their socks to regain it. Wouldn't it be easier then, for the government to dissolve the people and elect another?'

B.B.

The events lead him to rework a play on the Tui (corruptible intellectuals) in the guise of an oriental tale: *Turandot or the Congress of the Whitewashers.*

Brecht disguised as Stalin.

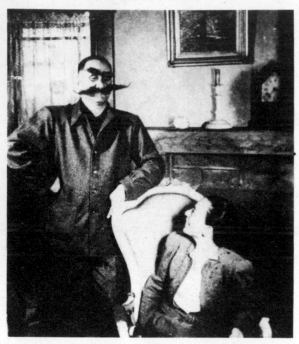

In 1955 he receives the Stalin Peace Prize in Moscow. In retaliation his plays are no longer staged in the West.

They're making cold war on him.

Brecht's last years are passed in almost 'Galilean' reclusiveness. He spends a lot of time in the country at his Buckow house. He works by the stop-watch. In East Berlin, the Brechts settle down about 10 minutes away from their theatre in the Chausseenstrasse (where the Archives are today) opposite the Huguenot cemetery. From his office, Brecht can see the tomb of Hegel.

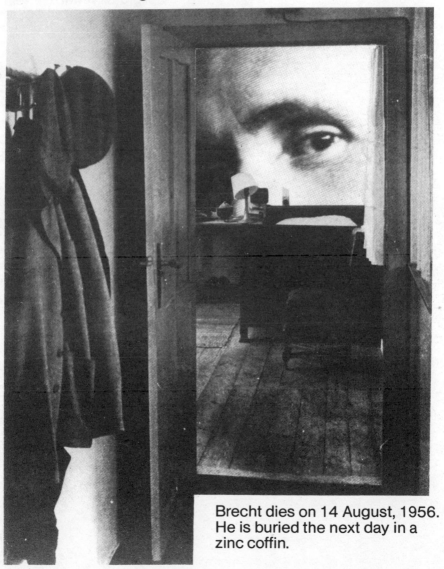

Brecht dies on 14 August, 1956. He is buried the next day in a zinc coffin.

ACT 5:

1. Dario Fo
2. Roger Planchon
3. Georgio Strehler
4. Peter Stein

GLOSSARY

Epic. For Brecht, the term does not mean a literary genre (he talks of the epic drama and novel) but the critical attitude of the narrator to the fable. He tells the story and comments on the plot but does not identify with it. In this way, the reader or spectator is allowed to observe and to form an opinion while maintaining a critical distance. Brecht speaks of *epic theatre* from 1926 onwards, contrasting it particularly with naturalist and expressionist tendencies. He is to call it a *theatre of the scientific era*, transmitting practical knowledge and teaching materialist thought capable of exercising some influence over reality. Distancing is the key element.

Didactic (— play). Complementing his Marxist studies, Brecht writes a number of didactic exercises which do without both theatre and audience. Intended for amateur troupes of the Communist Youth, their object is to experiment with collective behaviour in order to link political action and moral reflection. The actor-spectator learns while teaching to cease being a consumer and to become productive.

Distancing (German: *Verfremdung*). A term of Hegelian origin used freely by Brecht after 1936 to designate certain epic procedures intended to suppress well-known and obvious features of character and stage procedure. With the latter thus rendered unfamiliar and surprising, the spectator is prevented from any instinctive identification and from confusing the drama with reality. To the extent that he then recognizes a situation as historic, the world will appear to him capable of transformation: 'Henceforth the theatre presents the world so that the spectator will take possession of it.' *Distancing effects* include interludes and songs to interrupt the plot, placards anticipating later events, prologues and epilogues, admonitions to the audience, gestures, metaphors, music, scenery, etc. Many of these effects are already to be found in Asian theatre and in medieval farce.

Social gestus. The sum of the movements, behaviour, facial expressions, language and intonation employed by an individual in relation to others and which reveal both his personality and his social position. 'Words and gestures can be replaced by other words and gestures without in any way altering the social gestus.'